MEL BAY PRESENTS

ON COMPETITIONS

Dealing With Performance STRESS

By Denis Azabagic

1 2 3 4 5 6 7 8 9 0

Table of Contents

I would like to thank my wife Eugenia Moliner for her support during my many years of attending music competitions. Her support and encouragement during the crucial moments helped me achieve my goals. When my spirit quivered she gave me strength. Thank you Eugenia!

The Concept of Music and Competitions

I started attending international competitions seriously when I was 18 years old. After a few years of competing I started to think about the purpose and meaning of music competitions. Some questions came to my mind, like: "How much sense is there in comparing two or more performances? Does winning a competition mean you are the best or does it make you a good player or a musician? Can art be compared at all?"

Well, after a while I think I have found some answers to those questions, at least answers that are good enough for me.

First of all, I think that it is not possible to compare certain things, like the music of Bach and Mozart! Very often people have asked me who my favorite composer is, and I am sure you have been asked the same question at some point. I can't answer a question like that. Throughout history, there have been many genius composers, and it is impossible to pick the best. However, how many times do we talk about who is our favorite guitarist, flutist, violinist, orchestra, etc? When you listen to a few players in a series of concerts, you talk to your friends and colleagues, and you discuss certain issues, such as what you liked and what not. Similarly at competitions, you can listen to others and say whom you liked and whom not.

We all compare things; it is in our nature to do so. In a competition, the same situation occurs, but there are a few people (the jury) who decide the whole game. How many times have I heard the opinions of people who listened to a competition and who were saying that jury was wrong, that they do not know what they are doing. I have been one of those people myself. The only time I would have nothing to say was when I would win. Yes, winning makes everything look very good. So, if we are to go to a competition, we have to accept the fact that there will be judges who will make the decisions whether we like them or not. They will compare all the performances they hear and give their opinion about them, the same as we would do. The difference is that what they say counts in the competition result. That does not, however, mean that they are right. All humans make mistakes and judging is also a very personal and subjective matter. Still, I think there is sense in competing. There are several points to which I would pay attention if I were a judge, or on the other hand, when I am competing:

- Timbre / tone quality
- Technique
- Choice of repertoire
- Musicality (a very touchy subject). This I would divide in two areas: being musically gifted and being musically educated.
- Stage presence

I will discuss all of these elements in the chapter "How to Prepare for the Competition."

Now, one more question that comes to my mind is: Why do we need to compete?

Well, there is no need, actually; it is a choice. To enter a competition and to go through all that it represents is really tough. It requires a lot of work, discipline, and energy to cope with the pressure competition creates. On the other hand, the prizes are the things we go for. Beside the prizes that consist of cash, CD recording contracts, or concerts, there is something that we all think of, and that is a prestige. There is a general opinion that competitions help you in building your career. I think that they do. In order to establish yourself in the performance world, you have to perform. Let me say that competitions are not the only way to establish yourself as a performer, but they definitely help. On the other hand, winning a competition or several of them is no guarantee whatsoever that one will have a successful career. For me there was a period of my life in which I was going to many, many competitions, from 1992 through 2000, and that is one period that brought me many good things, one of them being a certain recognition in the classical guitar world. Still, I am convinced that if I don't keep fighting for my career all the competitions that I won will not help. It is great to win a competition and put that in our bio. That certainly helps later when we want to get concerts. Even if one does not win, playing in the competition is an opportunity where other people who can later help our career can notice us.

The bottom line is that competitions help in establishing one's name. Once again I have to say that they definitely are not the only way to make a performing career. There are other ways as well, and one should not be discouraged at all if he or she does not have a success at a competition and is led to believe that he (she) is not cut out for this profession. There are so many elements that come together for one to win a prize at a competition. For some people the competition environment is such a negative situation that everything falls apart. On the other hand, those same people perform extraordinarily well in concerts. Concerts and competitions are in some ways opposite situations. In the first, people come to hear you and enjoy; in the other, you are judged and criticized.

Apart from benefiting if you win a prize at the competition, there are other elements that we take home even if the experience seems totally negative. I think that there are quite a number of people that come to competitions and are not aware of the things in their playing that could be much better or some things that are even wrong. I remember once a judge told me that I play very well but too soft, that I cannot play just for myself but it has to be for the audience. I was very surprised. I thought I had played loud enough! Some time after that I realized that I could actually play with more sound and get a much better dynamic range. Sometimes it is the guitar's fault. Some people deny the fact that they do not have such a great instrument, because they paid a significant amount for it. If they hear the same comment from different people, maybe they will decide to face that fact and get a better instrument. Also there are reversed situations, where some players complain about the instrument, but the problem is really somewhere in their technique.

On occasion you can find talented young people studying in one place and performing in an area where everyone just keeps saying how good he or she plays. That tends to create an impression in that young person that he or she is the best and it could be difficult to face disappointments later on. If we play in different places then we will be more realistic about forming an opinion about ourselves. The truth is that there are so many good players around the world, and our town, state, province, or country is not the whole world. Performing in many places gives us a chance to hear new things and to learn.

I think it would be very beneficial to hear the judge's opinions and to reflect on them. I remember receiving the jury's notes from a Concert Artist Guild competition in New York, where I had played in the semi-finals, but didn't make it to the finals. I received the judge's notes on my performance a few months after the competition. It was really interesting to read them. I took some of them into account and reflected on them, while others I dismissed. All the notes were anonymous. I think this is a great idea. It gives the competitor a chance to get feedback on his or her playing. Given time to "cool off" after a competition for a few weeks, and not looking at the situation with the emotions that are present after a disappointing result, one can be more objective. Again I say one should know what to accept and what to reject. Once I received an E-mail from someone who attended the Guitar Foundation of America International Guitar Competition, asking me for an opinion on his playing in the semi-final round. I didn't hear the semi-finals so I could not tell him anything. This is just one example of someone looking for feedback on their playing. It is important to realize that at competitions you can get new and fresh ideas and opinions from people whose opinions you value. These opinions can be different from those we usually hear from our teacher, friends and other persons who are usually around us. On the other hand, you might hear the same things your teacher was telling you, thus helping you realize even better some things you should pay attention to.

All these reflections on our playing can be obtained elsewhere, at master-classes for example. The point that I am trying to make is, try to get the most out of a music competition. Competitions can be very pleasant or very frustrating experiences, but they can definitely give you a valuable experience.

Choosing a Competition

Once you have decided to enter a competition, you have to choose which of the many competitions you should participate in.

The first competition I attended was in 1982 or 1983. I was 10 or 11 and this competition was called the Republic Competition for music pupils and students of Bosnia and Herzegovina. In the former Yugoslavia we had these competitions every three or four years, and the students from music schools or academies would prepare for it. First, we would go to the Republic Competition and then the first prize winners would go to the Federal Competition of Yugoslavia. Something similar takes place in the U. S., where students compete first in competitions for a certain area of the country (Midwest, East Coast, etc.) and then advance to National level. The competition we had in the former Yugoslavia was also divided in to several categories according to the age. There were seven categories, I believe.

Back then everything was kind of predetermined. There was only that one competition (and another festival) and I did not have to think much about which competition to take part in. Besides, I was too young to make those decisions by myself, my teacher did that.

I also attended several international student competitions (festivals) in Italy and Greece where I won first prizes. I participated in those competitions during my high school years (14-17). I would strongly encourage students to participate in such competitions as well, and not to wait until it comes time for the "big ones".

It was a different story when I wanted to go to international competitions. There are so many guitar competitions and the way I chose which to go to might seem too pragmatic and materialistic: I looked for the competition with the best prizes. That is the reason I never went to Italy. The competitions there were usually well below other competitions in terms of prize compensations. Once I considered entering the competition in Alessandria, Italy, but something else came along.

When deciding, I was taking into account not only the first prize but all other prizes as well. The costs that I would incur in going to a competition were also part of my decision. Some competitions offered accommodations with local families ("René Bartoli" Competition in Aix en Provence, France; "Printemps de la Guitarre" in Walcourt, Belgium), which meant that the costs of attending these competitions were significantly lower. The "Francisco Tárrega" competition in Benicasim, Spain would pay the hotel bill for all participants for the first round and for all semi-finalists for the whole duration of the competition. In addition, semi-finalists were compensated with a certain amount of money (50,000 Pts / US $275). Furthermore, at this competition each finalist who did not get any prize (1st, 2nd, prize of the public or the special prize for the best interpretation of a work by Tárrega) was given 100,000 Pts / US $550, as compensation for being a finalist.

Sometimes in a competition it happens that a finalist gets nothing. When I won the "Manufacturas Alhambra" competition in Alcoy, Spain, the first prize was excellent and the 2nd and 3rd prize were not very significant. As there were five people in the final, two of them were left without any compensation for their merit. I mentioned this deficiency to the organizing committee and I believe that the next edition of competition featured a small award for finalists who did not win any of the main prizes.

So, for myself, those were the criteria by which I chose which competition to attend. However, I think that there are other criteria that can exist depending on which stage of development a student or a player is in. What I mean is that it is not necessary to wait until one feels that he or she has reached the peak of development (which actually never comes) in order to start entering competitions. One can participate at a competition in order to get experience for future competitions. Maybe the results in the first few competitions will not be so encouraging, but keep in mind that the experience that you gain from it will serve you well in the future, when you might be better prepared, more mature, and so on. The only way to know how to handle a competition is to take part in one. Having this in mind, then, we can approach choosing a competition with different criteria than mine.

If the objective is to gain experience, it would be good to take part in a competition which is not of the highest international level. There are a few sources where you can find out about competitions. Universities usually get information about competitions and your teachers also will know about some of them. You can also look in magazines that are related to your instrument, as well as on the Internet. At the end of this book I will provide a list and sources for some international guitar competitions. *Musical America* (published in the U. S.) is a great source for listings, not only for competitions but also for many other subjects related to music (foundations, schools, etc.). In many countries the Ministries of Education and Culture (or a similar governmental body) will have information about competitions. If you are trying to get information about foreign countries, get in touch with their embassies in your home country and address the cultural attaché of that embassy.

The best way to learn about a particular competition is to ask people who have participated at that competition. When people ask me about the level of some competition I find it difficult to assess. I would say that the required pieces could give you an idea of what kind of players the competition is trying to attract. Harder pieces naturally would suggest that the level would be higher. On the other hand, the lack of very difficult required pieces would not necessarily mean that the competition would have a "lower" level. Maybe the prizes are so desirable that they insure participation of very good performers.

Rehersal with orchetra for finals in Concurso Internacional de Guitarra
"Francisco Tarrega", Benicasim, Spain-1993.

Repertoire of Selection

Selection of repertoire is the next step in our competition endeavor. In the competitions in which I took part, I encountered very different requirements, ranging from those that would have a very selective program to those that do not have any required piece at all. I remember that the ARD Competition in Munich, Germany in 1993 was one of the most difficult for me in terms of the required program. During the course of the competition, which lasted four rounds, competitors had to play all different musical forms and styles: studies, sonatas, tremolo, original pieces, transcriptions, concerto, and music from Baroque, Classical and contemporary styles. This was not just a guitar competition, but rather a music competition (guitar was only one category among others) and this fact was reflected in the program required by the organization. Each instrument was competing in its own category, but high standards were applied to every category. A very similar program was required at another competition I took part in, in the town of Markneukirchen, Germany.

On the other hand, there were competitions where the required pieces were not so hard. For example the "Manufacturas Alhambra" competition in Alcoy, Spain had only one required piece, and it was not too difficult (I competed there twice). The rest of the program was free, with the rule that several stylistic periods had to be represented in the program. The "Andrés Segovia" competition in Palma de Mallorca in Spain had no required pieces at all. We only had to play pieces from two or three different periods. The "Jacinto e Inocencio Guerrero" competition in Madrid, Spain focuses on repertoire by Spanish composers throughout the different periods; the "Francisco Tárrega" competition in Benicasim, Spain, of course pays attention to music of Francísco Tárrega (his music is required in every round). In some competitions there would be a set piece, which was either specially written for that competition, as in the "Printemps de la Guitarre" in Walcourt, Belgium where a piece for orchestra and guitar would be commissioned for the final round.

Sometimes there are competitions which have two categories: guitar and composition for guitar. The winning composition becomes a "set piece" for the next year's guitar competition. Such is the case with a few competitions that I know of: the "Andrés Segovia" competition in La Herradura, Spain, "Citta de Alessandria" in Alessandria, Italy, and the Guitar Foundation of America competition in the USA. This I find very significant, because it encourages young composers to write for guitar and consequently it enriches the repertoire. Sometimes this can be a frustrating experience, too, when players have to learn and perform a piece that makes no sense to anyone at all. Yes, I have experienced that a number of times. That is one of the downsides of competitions—learning music that you will probably never play again. Everything has a price. Those are the most difficult pieces for me. When I play something that makes no sense to me, I do not know what to do with it. What then? Act, I guess. Let's call it musical acting....

Back to repertoire for competition. After reviewing the required pieces, the selection of free repertoire is extremely important. There are certain pieces that are meant to be played in concerts which are not suitable for competition because they lack a certain seriousness. For example, very often I would hear someone perform a piece in competition that is of a more "popular" style, the kind of piece that audiences like to hear in a concert. The only justification I would find for including such a piece in the program would be in the event that there is a prize awarded by the audience, and one wants to win it. Apart from that, the pieces we select as our free program have to show variety in our playing, both from a technical as well as a musical point of view. I made a mistake about this once in '92, when I played a piece I liked; a jury member, (Leo Brouwer), later told me that I had made a bad choice and that my mistake had cost me a better placement.

Let's say that in one round of the competition a study (etude) is required; for the free program I would then choose a piece that would be of a deeper musical language, especially if the study is written in a more virtuosic style. In every instrument's technique there are so many different aspects. Talking about the guitar, we have arpeggios, tremolo, slurs, harmonics, scale-like passages, sound production quality, etc. So, many times I have seen people "blown away" by someone who plays fast scales, yet his or her sound was very harsh and "naily." I think that beautiful tone should be a very important element in playing. This does not mean that we shouldn't ever have a harsh and "naily" sound, only sometimes!

Besides all of the different technical elements that we can think of when choosing a repertoire, we also have to be aware that there are many musical aspects we have to think of. Music from different periods is one important element to have in mind, because the different character of the pieces can make our program more interesting and varied. It is important to think of all of the human emotions which can be reflected in the music: joy, melancholy, sadness, anger, happiness, disappointment, etc. There is always a story behind every piece, how it was composed, what inspired the composer to write it. Maybe it is based on a real life story; maybe it is a musical description of some story or book the composer read. We can also put our own story behind a piece, and it is important to play music that allows us to use our imaginations.

So don't think that it is enough to simply play well, or that we can choose any piece we want to play in competition. Maybe we can do this in a concert, but I once had a jury member tell me, "I have heard two people who played very well. One of them played an easier piece and it was so beautiful I felt bad that I had to choose between these two players. But I had to; this is a competition, so I had to keep in mind that the other played a more difficult piece that carried more points. If I heard them in a concert I would not have to make a choice, but here I had to vote for the one who played the more difficult piece."

I had another experience related to program variety in a competition, this time at the McMahon International Music Competition in Lawton, Oklahoma in June 2000. I participated in that competition as a one of the six finalists chosen from a tape round. I was the only guitarist. The program requirement for the final round was to play a recital. I decided to play a recital program that I had performed nearly sixty times in a seven-month period, during my Guitar Foundation of America tour. After playing this program so many times in a short period of time, I thought it would be a good idea to play it at the competition where I would be compared to other instrumentalists and singers. I played very well, and shared 2nd prize with a cellist. I was really happy knowing that this was not a guitar competition, but rather a music competition. One of the jury members told me that if I had played a more diversified program, including maybe a piece by J. S. Bach, there could have been two first prizes. My program was made up of Spanish and South American composers, most of them from the 20th century. I was aware of this when I submitted my program, and had made a decision to go with the program I was very comfortable with instead of making it more varied.

Let me tell you about another incident that occurred in competition in Markneukirchen, Germany in 1997. In one of the rounds there was a requirement for a Sonata. In the competition brochure several composers were listed as possible choices. I chose one of them, Manuel Maria Ponce, and his piece *Sonatina Meridional*. I did not think at the time of the fact that Sonata and Sonatina were actually two different things, although the sonata form is clearly present in Sonatina Meridional. Anyway, after I played my round, the jury wanted to disqualify me because I played a sonatina and not a sonata. After a few agonizing hours the decision was made that I would stay in the competition because the organizing committee had accepted my repertoire list a few months before, and the jury had no authority to disqualify me once I was accepted to compete. UUUUFFFF! I ended up getting a third prize there.

Be very careful when you read the competition rules (look who's talking!). Respect the fact that sometimes rules require a certain edition of the piece and that the jury can take it into account if you do not play the required edition. Occasionally members of the jury may try to disqualify you on the basis of these "silly" non-musical considerations.

In some competitions the final round includes a performance of a concerto, either with orchestra or with piano accompaniment. I will address this issue in the chapter, "Final Round with Concerto."

How to Prepare for a Competition

Naturally, after you've selected a program for a competition there comes practice.

I do not approach preparation and practice of these pieces any differently than those that I would prepare for any other occasion. The music is the same, no mater where it will be played. Sometimes we have to play pieces that we are not familiar with and have never heard of. In that instance, I try to find a recording of the piece and listen just to have a better idea about it. I also try to get to work on the pieces as soon as I can, so that I have some time to allow the piece to "mature". What I mean is that I do not like to have the piece prepared and ready just before the competition starts. I personally prefer to have enough time so that after I practice it, I can put it aside and not play it for some time. Later, I come back to it just before the competition begins.

In the first chapter of this book I said I would discuss a few elements which I take into consideration when playing and practicing. Here they are again:

TIMBRE / TONE QUALITY

In my experience as a guitarist, which started when I was 6 and continues unbroken to the present day, timbre/tone quality has come up many times as a very controversial subject. I personally like to take care of the sound; I try to establish a warm, pleasant tone that will be my basic timbre. From there I can go and try more colors, from even darker and very sweet tone to a bright, harsh, "naily" sound and from *sul tasto* to *ponticello*. I have heard many players who play very well, but whose sound in my opinion was not nice. It was not properly taken care of! I started having doubts about this after I heard many players who have a rather "harsh" sound. Then I approached some people and friends who are guitar aficionados. I asked them what it is they like about guitar, what it is that attracts them to this instrument more than any other. Their answer was the SOUND of the guitar! I think that the guitar has the ability to create a beautiful and sweet sound unlike any other instrument. I am not saying that other instruments cannot produce beautiful sounds, but I am saying that the guitar has particular color which can be extraordinarily beautiful if explored.

Think of it this way: I am sure all of us have heard the great "Three Tenors," Pavarotti, Domingo and Carreras. They are all great singers, but when I hear Pavarotti's voice it just freezes me with its simple extraordinary beauty. On the other hand, it seems strange to hear any of them sing popular music in their concerts. For example, I remember listening to Carreras singing the famous song "Singing in the Rain." It doesn't work! The same goes for Pavarotti's performance of songs by U2 at his concerts. I think there is a voice and color for "Nesun Dorma" as well as there is definitely a color for "Singing in the Rain." Maybe easier to understand for us guitarists would be the color of flamenco guitar. When you hear a classical guitarist playing flamenco it probably seems too "tidy," too "careful." Flamenco requires a certain type of sound typical of that music, just as the classical style needs its type of sound. I took as examples singers and guitarists to try to make my point on this issue; similar examples, however, could be given with other instruments and styles of music in which those instruments are involved.

TECHNIQUE

Technique is something of incredible importance to any performer, but it never can be an objective in itself. It is a tool, a vehicle in which our music travels. The better the vehicle the smoother the ride will be. If we only display the technique then the vehicle will be circling around without taking the listeners on a journey to any special place. On the other hand if a player is musical and his or her technique is not good enough, the music will suffer. Technique is a very complex combination of many different elements. Acquisition of good technique is a long process requiring years of hard work, discipline and commitment. How can we develop good technique? The best way is to find an excellent teacher and study hard.

MUSICALITY

As I said earlier this is a very touchy subject. I think this is the source of major disagreement among those who listen to (or judge) music. I also mentioned in the opening chapter that I would divide musicality into two areas: being musically gifted and being musically educated.

Now that I am starting to teach more and more (master classes, festivals, and at the university level) I see this distinction between education and talent more clearly then before. Often I hear students who have a great temperament and musical talent, but they lack a deeper understanding of the piece from an analytical point of view. It is easier to work with those students because temperament or talent cannot be learned or taught, but the teacher can mold it or help it evolve and grow. I would call this kind of student musically gifted and that is something one carries inside. The gift alone however is not enough. Then comes musical education, those numerous things we are learning in schools and universities. We can also learn a tremendous amount outside of schools and established institutions.

First, let's go back to schools. We have all studied (or are studying) solfeggio, harmony, counterpoint, musical analysis, musical form, music styles, historic periods in music and art in general, etc. All these elements must come into the picture when we start working on a piece. What we see in the piece, and how clearly we can see it and recognize it makes a huge difference in our playing. Do we know where the melody is, where it begins, where and how it ends? What rhythm is the melody set in, and do we respect that rhythm or we take too much "artistic liberty" with it (trying to compensate for fingers which are not able to move fast enough or stretch enough)? Is the melody in a single voice or are we playing a polyphonic piece where the melody is hidden in many voices? Do we see it then? Do we follow the tempo markings, dynamics and other indications written in the score? Do we understand the foreign language in which those markings are written, or are we too busy just figuring out where to place our fingers to play those notes? Do we understand the harmonic structure of the piece and use dynamics and energy to help the harmonic progression or resolution? Do we understand the form of the piece, whether it is a fantasia, prelude, fugue, sonata, dance, song, suite, etc.? Are we able to recognize what the composer is doing with a phrase, how he shapes it, turns it around, breaks it into smaller bits or motives, and then plays with them again, putting them into sequences, changing the tonality, putting musical material close together, changing the texture, rhythm, tempo, etc.? These are only a few of these questions and points which we learn with time. I remember being a student and having lessons with people who inspired me from the beginning, so much that I would say to myself: "Oh my God, how many things there are to learn!" I still have the same feeling.

Musical or artistic talent is of course essential for music, but it remains only talent if our brain is not engaged in a partnership with it. The combination of these two elements is a truly remarkable union.

STAGE PRESENCE

Self-assuredness on stage is something all of us have to learn. There are a few "rules" of behavior on the stage. First of all, we should know that what we do is a performing art, and it is important to transmit something to the audience even before we start playing. Our little walk from the stage door to center stage is the first thing judges and audiences will see. So let that walk be confident and strong (not a military style, though). This little walk is not your everyday kind of walk. In a way, it is a parade so put a smile on your face. I think the smile is very important. The point of playing is to enjoy ourself, and a smiling face is definitely a reflection of enjoyment. Of course, we are nervous when we have to walk out on stage and play. It is not an easy thing to do, but we should keep all the problems with nerves and such to ourselves. Audiences or judges have to feel as if this is our daily routine and that we are filled with pleasure and confidence.

If you have to adjust the chair for your performance, first acknowledge and bow to the audience and then do the chair. I have seen a player come out on stage without greeting the audience before adjusting the chair, bending over it and showing his rear to the audience! Please face the audience even when adjusting the chair and most definitely turn your rear to the wall, not towards people's faces!

There are many good ways to bow. Your teacher can help you with that. It is just a question of practice; with a few tries I am sure anyone can get it. At some festivals my colleagues and I take all the students out for a little bowing practice on the day of the concert. It is really easy. Just have someone help you with it. You can either look good or not so good on stage—it is up to you. Do not disregard stage presence; it is a very important element of the whole "show."

MENTAL PREPARATION/MEMORIZATION

There is one thing I paid more attention to when I prepared for competition than I would for a concert. That is mental preparation and memorization of the program.

For some time now I have been thinking about memorization and the way our brains memorize. During my guitar studies and development I have heard of several different ways of memorizing pieces. Some suggest memorizing the actual music, as in having a photographic memory of the score. I have managed to memorize very little this way. The way I memorize is to remember the positions of every note on the fretboard. I was wondering why this works better for me. I came to the following conclusion:

Let's say we need to remember one note: F♯ (the one on the first string). In order to memorize how to play this note we have to remember the note (its pitch), the finger with which we press, and the string on which the note is played. This particular note we can play on three different strings (even four), so just knowing that we have to play an F♯ is not enough. The fingers remember where they have to press, and this is actually what we practice over and over again, the movement, not the information that we read in the first place. The danger is that we start relying too much on the fingers remembering where to go, and when we play in a stressful situation (competition, exam, concert), then sometimes the fingers will not know where to go. Why does this happen?

My guess is that there are two different ways in which our brain remembers. One is by repeating and storing that information in some part of the brain that is beyond our consciousness. I would call it memorization of repeated motion. The other way is the one we do not practice so much and is essential when the stress comes along. That is the part in which all our thinking takes place, where we ask ourselves too many questions while we play, and think of too many things that are negative for our playing. How many times has it happened to any of us that we stopped in the middle of the piece and had no idea of what comes next? In my experience as a teacher, I see students who come for a lesson and when I ask them to play from a certain spot, they can't do it, even with the score. They have to find a familiar starting point for their fingers. This suggests that there is no relation between written music (score) and playing (motions).

When one starts learning a piece from the score, the brain processes the information and the piece is learned as a set of motions. Then the first information input, which came as a score, is forgotten. The fingers become the leaders in the whole process of playing, and the brain is left in second place. The brain should have the lead and the fingers should follow. This holds true to a certain extent, but it has to be part of the learning and memorizing process. What I mean is that after good memorization of the piece, we can then "let go" and let our hands do their job without constant supervision of the brain. In order to get to this stage in which we can "let go" we have to make sure that we have really memorized the piece with this conscious part of the brain. This is what I do when I want to make sure that I memorized the music well.

I would go through my whole repertoire in my head a day before I had to play. If I travel I often use that time to do my memory exercise. The night before a performance when I go to bed, I do the same. How? I visualize the motions of my left-hand fingers from the beginning of the piece to the end. Every motion, every fret and finger that moves to that fret. The picture I visualize in my head is the same picture that I see when I play and observe my left hand. It is as if I had a camera on my head recording every motion. Then I play that film in my head. Sometimes there are problems. I just don't know what is coming next, what the next motion is, or the next fret. I call this a "trouble spot." Then I go to my score and check that spot. I do all of this without the guitar in hand.

I do one other thing with the guitar that improves memorization and makes me more confident. I play the piece extremely slow and I think ahead of my fingers, what is coming next, which note, which finger. All of these exercises are very difficult and tiring but believe me, they are incredibly useful. I accept this process and these exercises as a part of the whole concept of practice, something that I have to do. Just as I have to read the piece, practice it and learn it, the memorization exercises are part of the whole process the piece has to go through before being performed on the stage.

Now, all of these measures are extremely important and useful, but have to be done in their time and left behind once we step on the stage.

IMAGINATION

There is something else I have to think about before the actual performance; that is the music itself.

Making music for me is like telling a story. Each story has its beginning, development, climax and ending. The storyteller takes written material, which he first has to read the same as a musician has to read a music score. The letters have to be identified, then letters make words, words make small phrases, those phrases make sentences, paragraphs, chapters, parts, and the whole story. What about the symbols: ., ", ', !, ?, ;, and ( )? All of these symbols help articulate the sentence the same as indications for dynamics, tempo, etc., help shape a musical phrase.

Once a storyteller has read the material which he has to tell on the stage and has understood all the symbols, letters, pronunciations, etc., there is still more to be done so that those who listen will find the story enjoyable. The story has to be interpreted. He has to live the story in his imagination, to give the story life, direction, excitement when it needs it, to speak in surprising ways, to shout, to whisper, to cry, to laugh- all while telling the story. If he doesn't do that, we might like the story, but we would not enjoy it nearly as much as we would if he had put all of his emotional expression into it.

For me it's the same with music. We can learn all the indications that come in the score, notes, rhythm, tempo marks etc. put it all together and execute with great speed and accuracy, but then what? It is still empty. Imagination helps us make a story from the piece of music, a story that will be told in a different language, not the spoken one, but one that is played and sung. This process can be learned and practiced as well. Of course, one cannot become musical by practicing if he or she has no talent for it. What I mean here is that it is possible to practice the art of interpretation and the feelings and musicality we have inside can gradually be brought to the surface. Little by little, imaginative interpretation helps to overcome stage fright. For me, this process started many, many years ago and it is still ongoing. Each of us has an inner world that expands with the things we experience over time. With each year that passes in our lives our experience grows and so does our inner world. For many, it is very difficult to share this inner world, but music is one of the best ways to reflect what we have inside.

How many times have we practiced at home alone, enjoying travel to any place we choose through our imaginations? We can imagine playing in the most famous concert hall in the world, or the most remote place – on a mountain top or a beautiful beach, or anywhere. These are exactly the same places we want to go to when we are on the stage performing in front of an audience. Let's leave our body and hands playing the sounds and our mind and soul can be somewhere else. Dare to do that, to enter the other world, the other dimension, and you will open the door for those who are listening to you so they can follow.

As I said, this process cannot be practiced if one does not possess an imagination in the first place. I think we all have imagination, some more and some less, but the object is to reveal one's imagination and feelings. If we play at home and are able to use imagination, then the same can be done on the stage. It is a question of practicing, taking time and believing that it can be done.

PLAYING IN FRONT OF AN AUDIENCE, TESTING THE PROGRAM AND FIXING TROUBLE SPOTS

A very good tool for overcoming stage fright is a staged performance. The only way to learn how to deal with this situation is to put ourselves in it as much as we can. So, before any important performance event whether it be a competition, exam or concert, it is very useful to do *try-outs*. Even if those try-outs are just in front of a few friends, they create a situation similar to the one we will be facing. While studying in The Netherlands I would often use the performance class to rehearse the program I would be playing in a competition. Sometimes while playing I would have memory slips or make other kinds of errors. That made me feel bad and in a way would shake my confidence. I had thought the program should go smoothly because I was about to perform at the competition. When that did not happen I felt discouraged. I did not see at that point that this experience was actually a great help.

Those trial performances showed me where my weak spots were, and which parts required a little more attention. I would then work more on those spots, dedicate more time to them to memorize them better, or even change some fingerings. Sometimes there are passages that we play with certain fingerings that seem to work at home, but are not quite reliable when we become a little nervous. If that is the case, change them, and try to find those that would work in any situation.

It is generally said that we do not learn from good experiences but from the bad ones. I think in great part that is true. If the experience is bad we try to change things so that we do not suffer the same circumstances again. On the other hand, a good experience helps us build up confidence. So, take it this way: If the try-out goes well, feel good about it and think you can do the same thing when the time comes to perform again. On the other hand, if the try-out goes poorly, feel good again! You had a chance to run the program and see where your trouble spots are, you get the chance to fix them, and that is what the try-outs are for– to make mistakes; better to make mistakes during the try-out then during the real performance, right? It is always better to have a positive but critical attitude, rather then a negative one full of doubts. Doubts are good to a certain extent, but there comes a point where one should say, "Enough, I am not paying attention to the doubts about this project any more."

The try-outs could be used not just for trying out the program, but for preparing your whole attitude towards the performance. You can do the same things during the try-out day that you would during the day of the actual performance. Not only could you, but you should. For example, if you do too many things the day of a try-out, you will probably be tired and not in optimal condition to perform. If you practice a lot on the day of the try-out, again you will be tired. So, in order to get the most out of the try-out, treat it the same as the actual performance.

See also the chapter: The Day of the Performance.

FOCUS AND STATE OF MIND DURING THE COMPETITION

Once you get to the competition there will be many things that are happening around you and inside of your head that will distract you from your goal. I am sure it happens to many of us that we read the resumés of all the competitors, their programs and times of performances, the jurors' qualifications, and so on. How does it make us feel to read about some competitor with quite an impressive list of accomplishments or a list of prizes he has won? Then we notice that the teachers of some competitors are on the jury and of course that makes us think even more about the whole situation. We start questioning the fairness of the competition and judging. We also think about when we are scheduled to play and that brings up the following questions: Is it better to play in the beginning or at the end? Does the jury need some time to "warm up"? I mean, if I play at the very beginning, maybe the jury won't be

With my friend Zoran Dukic (second left) and wife Eugenia Moliner at Concurso Internacional de Guitarra "Francisco Tárrega", Benicasim, Spain-1993 (My wife is telling people how bad I played).

"into it" yet, maybe they won't notice my playing no matter what I do? If I play at the end, will the jury be so tired and bored of listening to the same piece more then 50 times that they will not even listen to me carefully? What if I have to play just after someone I know is very good? That might really make me sound mediocre.

Does any of this sound familiar to you?

I asked myself all of these questions. Did it help me? Not at all. After a while I started to narrow my attention to the things which could be under my control. I realized that the only thing I have control over is my body, my mind, my soul, and my playing. I could not change any of the other factors: the panel of judges, time of performance, other competitors and their playing, or the decision of the judges. None of that could be under my influence. The only thing I had certain control over was my playing. So, I tried to focus my energy on my playing and take my mind off all those other things that went through my head.

At the last few competitions I attended, the only thing I needed to know was when and where I had to play and when I could come to warm up. I would spend my time practicing, resting and doing other things that would take my mind off the competition, like reading, watching TV, walking, etc. The best thing to take my mind off the impending competition was to read a really interesting book, a novel. I would also go to lunch with friends and try to talk about other things besides the competition (although that was difficult).

To Listen or Not to Listen to the Other Competitors?

During competition I would not listen to other players before my performance. I would do that only *after* I had played. It is good to listen to the others in order to assess the levels of the competition and individual competitors. This also helps us determine where we stand in comparison, and as I said before, helps us learn new things. My advice to everybody is not to listen to anyone until your performance is over. Even if you are the last to play, don't listen. You can hear some players in the next round; you don't have to hear them in the first round. Listening to others before our own performance makes us think too much. One starts thinking about how this person played a particular piece. He played it better then I think I play it, or he or she played faster, or slower, or did this and that, and on and on.

Nothing of this nature helps us play better. On the contrary, it takes our focus away from where it has to be, and that is on our playing. This is especially true of those who are inexperienced in competition. A person like that could be easily intimidated by someone else's playing or even by their attitude. Stay in your own world until you have done your job. There will be plenty of time to find out all the other things you want to know. When I won the GFA competition in Montreal, Canada, I did not hear any of the other competitors. I was thinking that I came to do my job and that was to play the best I could, and that was it. Nothing else mattered. I did not even know who was in the jury. I knew I would find that out later. That kind of focus helped me in making the most out of my playing. Of course I did not have this same experience when I started competing. I was doing too many things in the beginning that I later eliminated from my routine. The GFA competition was the 30th-something competition for me; after that many competitions I had a better picture of how to handle the whole competition process.

Receiving prize in Concurso Internacional de Guitarra "Francisco Tárrega"
in Benicasim, Spain 1995

The Day of the Performance

One of the most familiar feelings to me is that of tension on the day of the performance. I used to have a feeling as if my insides wanted to come out. It is not a pleasurable feeling, but with time I learned to accept it instead of fighting it. I used to wish for the day when that feeling would go away, but now I am aware that it will never happen. I think that we always have goals for the future and if these are things that we desire and consider important, then we will always have a feeling of responsibility to achieve them. If I have to play in a situation where I have already proven myself, then the next time the level of responsibility is lower and with it the tension is also reduced. On the other hand, if I were approached to play at a very important festival or concert hall, or to appear as a soloist with an important orchestra, then I would expect my "tension-responsibility" feeling to be intensified. Now I try to welcome that feeling because I realized it is a part of what I am doing. I do not try to fight it and pretend that it will go away, although I wish it would. As I progress as a guitar player and musician, I have learned how to cope with that feeling better and better every time it arises. The point is, if you feel nervous on the day of the performance, do not feel bad about it, but rather accept it, even talk and joke about it. The important thing is to maintain the focus on the performance.

My reaction to winning the 1st prize, audience award and special prize for best interpretaion of work by Tárrega at Concurso Internacinal de Guitarra "Francisco Tárrega", Benicasim, Spain-1995

Being nervous in the face of an impending competition or performance makes us doubt very easily, and it could happen that we might practice too much. You have to trust yourself and know that too much practicing on the day of the performance can do more harm than good. It would be nice if you could have an alarm in your head which tells you that no matter what, you have to trust yourself and not play all day long. It is tempting! I would suggest a one-hour practice session and a warm up session before performance, which also should not be too long. I use to take a long warm up sessions, up to an hour and half (not playing all that time of course) in order to go through all of my pieces, at least partially. Now I see that this is not necessary; forty-five minutes to one hour is plenty. The day of the performance I used to practice one hour in the morning, not very hard, just lightly going through the program. (Nowadays, very often I do not practice at all on the day of a performance, but just warm up before the concert.)

The rest of the day I try to do other things that take my mind off what is ahead. I like to read a book, or watch something interesting on TV, take a walk, or play some video game (not too much though because you can make your fingers tired or even hurt them). If my mind goes to the performance, then I try to think about the music, all the things that are related to the piece that help me make music. I try to block all the thoughts related to pressure, the jury, self-doubt, etc. I know that those "negative thoughts" come and I just keep taking my mind to where I want it to be. It is hard, but with time and experience it gets easier.

It is very important for me to have a very restful day when I have to perform. It takes a lot energy and focus to do a good performance, and usually after the performance I am very tired. So, I like to have a lot of energy when I go to the stage. That means being rested, and I do that by taking a good afternoon nap. I try to sleep about one hour after lunch. Now, if the performance is in the morning or in the afternoon, as it can be so many times at competitions, then it is important to have an early night and not to stay out late partying (which can happen easily at some competitions).

I do not like to be hungry when I am on stage either, as it makes it more difficult for my fingers to stay warm. Some people have told me that they prefer to be hungry while playing because it helps their concentration! Well, we are all different. I like to eat a light meal about an hour or hour and a half before the performance. It is also important to know which food is more likely to upset your stomach in a stressful situation. I wouldn't eat hot things for example, or anything too spicy. The rest is a matter of personal preference. I usually have a banana and chocolate available when I play (not on stage, of course). Eating some sugar helps, especially at the beginning of the performance. Do not exaggerate though, I have a friend who ate ten bananas the day of his performance! One banana is enough before the concert!

As the moment of performance approaches I try to keep my mind focused on music. All those ideas about imagination, inspiration, storytelling with the piece– those are the things I try to think about. The same thing goes during the performance. One can get into an incredible state of inspiration, but this doesn't occur all that frequently. In the beginning it can be a struggle to get ourselves away from where we physically are and enter that wonderful world of music, leaving our bodies where they are and going to that musical place with our mind and soul. Just believe in yourself and think that there are two voices in you, something like what we see in the movies: an angel on one shoulder and a devil on the other. Each of them is saying different things, and it is up to us to choose which one to listen to. So, listen to the voice that tells you that you can do it, even if that voice becomes weak; bring it to the fore by repeating the good things to yourself.

Even if you feel nervous your behavior must not show it. There is an element of acting in performance and every person who goes on the stage is a performer. What I mean is that actors, singers, and dancers are all performers as well and with that in mind every performance contains an element of acting. Our faces have to be smiling or at least conveying a pleasant and good feeling to the audience. Of course our expressions will change with the music, but that is what should lead our expressions- the music. Show confidence; it doesn't mater if it seems to you that you are faking it. Remember, stage appearance is very, very important, so take care of it. Do not make strange faces if you make a mistake. Just go on, and you will be surprised how many times our mistakes go unnoticed, especially when we manage to draw the audience into our world. Speaking of making faces and commenting on one's own mistakes, I have even seen people curse quite loudly when they made a mistake. What a horrible thing!

I always tell myself that music is all that matters, the music reaches beyond prizes, career, success, money, etc. MUSIC IS ALL THAT MATTERS.

THE JURY

The Jury is one of those things that we tend to think a lot about during a competition, and even before the competition. Many people have asked me what I think the jury is looking for at competitions. Some people think that they should play differently for a different kind of jury. I have always thought that it's not a good idea to change the way you play, no matter who is listening. You can never make everybody happy, so just stick to your concept and your playing will be convincing.

Very often competitors ask themselves what this or that person is doing in the jury. Certainly there are more qualified people who should be sitting there and judging instead of this person. I agree with that, but the fact is that sometimes, things work in a way that does not make a lot of sense. In the guitar world, it would be more likely to find someone not really qualified in a jury than in other music competitions. The classical guitar is a relatively young instrument and if it is easy to find a bad performer with certain exposure, then it is even easier to find a bad judge.

Another interesting thing about juries in the guitar world is that there are not really that many people around and we tend to see the same jurors in different competitions, or even worse, the same jury at the same competition over and over again. On the other hand we often see the same players at the same competitions as well. That is true (in my case for sure), but competitions are for young players to have a chance for exposure. The more competitions you attend, the better. One of the problems that I have seen in having the same jury at various competitions or at the same competition is that jury members may remember a player from a past competition and that might influence the decision in a current competition.

Let me explain: Let's say that a particular player does very well in a few competitions, then goes to another and has a bad day but still advances to the next round, even though there were people who really played better in that particular round. The explanation that I might give is that the jury members know this player *can* play better than they have just demonstrated and make their decision based on that fact. I think that this has happened to me, because sometimes I thought I wouldn't make it to the next round but I did; the only explanation I could give myself was that the members of the jury knew me from other competitions where I had played well. I do not think this scenario should occur but I am certain that it happens often. Then there is the opposite scenario, when you have played poorly a few times in the past and someone on the jury remembers you and already has an opinion of you, even before you play.

I have competed in Europe and the USA and I can speak only for these two parts of the world. I think that there are more people in Europe who are jury members at one point or another than in USA. Also, there are fewer competitions in the USA, even though it is a very big country. You really get the feeling that after participating in one competition three times you have gotten to know everyone! I also know that the organizers of competitions are concerned about finding new people to serve on the jury. The more famous players do not like to be on the juries because it is not a very rewarding job. Some competitions do not pay fees to the jurors, or they pay very little. Then it is much more fun to play a concert and have most of the people admiring you, rather than judging and making only a few, or very often only one person happy, and the rest of them miserable and "hating" you because of your, or worse, someone else's decision! Because jurors must listen to so many performances of the same piece, it really is a tough job; no wonder we do not see a great number of people doing it. One of the good things that I have seen in some juries is that they include musicians who are not guitarists, like conductors, composers, pianists, etc. This certainly creates more diversified juries.

Playing at the finals of III Concurso Internacional de Guitarra Alhambra in Alcoy, Spain-1996.

What about the jury members who have students competing in the same event? Should the students or former students be forbidden to participate in the competition if their teacher is on the jury? Should the jury member be forbidden to grant points to his or her student? My answer to both of these questions is no. No one should be denied acceptance to a competition if the teacher of that person will be in the jury, and neither should a jury member be denied a vote for his or her student. I think that we have to begin from the perspective of professionalism and fairness and assume that the jury that is hired will judge according to their professional and ethical standards. It is normal that a teacher will like the playing of someone he has taught. After all, if you teach someone you are showing the student how to play the way you think the instrument should be played. Then it is normal to like the performance of your students more than that of someone whom you did not teach who is performing differently. Now, there is a system that I have seen where the chances of too much favoritism could be lowered: Each member of the jury gives points for each performer. The highest and lowest scores are taken away and the rest is then taken in to account. It seems a reasonable system to me.

The greater the number of jury members, the better the situation is. Not only that, but recruiting the jurists from different backgrounds makes the judging more objective in my opinion.

Many times I have seen and I myself have been one of the angry competitors who felt that an injustice had been done. Let me only say that this is part of the game as well. You just go on to the next competition. Injustices don't only occur in competitions, but in life as well.

Cavatina Duo-Eugenia Moliner, flute and Denis Azabagic, guitar

Final Round with Concerto

At some competitions the final round includes a performance of a concerto with orchestra or with the accompaniment of a piano. The first time I performed with orchestra I must admit I felt a bit lost, not in terms of notes and beats, but I did not really know how to be a soloist. I remember expecting help from the conductor, or a bit of advice or encouragement, but I was very wrong. With time I have learned that the role of the soloist is the role of a leader; no matter how scared and nervous we might feel about performing in a final with orchestra, the fact is that we have to summon our courage and lead the whole orchestra.

Don't expect that you will always play with a good orchestra. It can happen that the orchestra is out of tune, speeding up in slow movements which is bad, and speeding up in fast movements, which is even worse!!!

Often times the players in the orchestra will learn their parts during rehearsals. At the first rehearsal you only think about keeping the things together and after the second rehearsal you can start thinking of musical issues. Do not be afraid to insist on the things you need in order to perform the piece better: your tempos, musical ideas, etc... Don't expect the conductor to know what you want if you do not tell him (and repeat it several times). Things always go better during the actual performance, and if you are into making music the conductor and the orchestra follow.

Bad things can happen too!!

I remember playing in the final one year at the "Francisco Tárrega" competition in Benicasim, Spain. I played "Fantasia para un Gentilhombre" by Joaquin Rodrigo. This is a very beautiful piece written in the form of a dialogue between guitar and orchestra, where there are a lot of solo guitar sections followed by orchestra section. In one movement I skipped two bars that I was supposed to play and went onto the following section. I did not realize that I had skipped the two bars and when the orchestra did not enter when I expected it I was amazed. I could not understand why the orchestra stopped playing. Then it came to me after a few moments and I realized that I had made a mistake and skipped a section. Nevertheless, the orchestra should not have stopped. Now, imagine the feeling of sitting in front of the whole theater and mumbling to the conductor where to pick up!!! Immediately my head filled with negative thoughts; I thought that everything was lost, but somehow I convinced myself that I had to go on as best I could and perform the rest of the piece as well as the solo piece. I did that and at least I got the audience award.

For us classical guitarists, it is very important to have good amplification when playing with an orchestra. If the jury cannot hear you they will not have anything to vote on!

So take time to do the sound check and make things work properly. It is really hard to play without amplification when playing with an orchestra, but you may be required to do just that. In Benicasim the prevailing opinion is that the guitar does not need amplification because the performance takes place in a small theatre. It is one thing to play solo, but another thing to play with at least 30 other instruments which are all more powerful than guitar in terms of volume, not to mention *tutti* segments! The only thing one can do in this situation is to think of *fortissimo* as the quietest dynamic level you should play!

There are situations where you will play a concerto but with a pianist replacing the orchestra. This is not nearly as enjoyable as playing with an orchestra, but still it is nice to play chamber music as opposed to playing solo all the time. A bad pianist, however, is worse than a bad orchestra. Once in La Herradura, Spain I played *Concierto de Aranjuez* by Rodrigo with a pianist. Imagine how this person was playing if he had to practice during the intermission of the final round, in front of an audience that did not leave during the break. Not only that, he had to play the concerto four times as there where four finalists. Unfortunately, I was the first on the program and that was the point where he barely knew the piece. By the fourth performer he managed to keep the tempo but when playing with me, he rushed so much at one point in the third movement that I gave up and stopped playing. I just could not handle that crazy tempo, but I caught on later. In addition, at the end of the first movement he replaced the eight bars of the closing section with the eight bars of the opening section! Can you imagine how I felt expecting what should come and instead I heard the beginning part? Just imagine the expression of surprise, amazement and disbelief on my face! That exact expression was repeated three more times by the other finalists. The pianist did the same thing four times, even after practicing during the intermission in front of the audience!

In other words, be prepared for anything!

Financing the Cost of Participation in a Competition

Many students face financial issues when deciding which competitions to attend. I have obtained financing for competitions from different sources. The conservatory where I studied in Rotterdam (The Netherlands) often helped me with travel expenses. Another organization in the same country (UAF) paid for a few of my competition trips as well. The UAF is an organization that helps foreign refugee students in The Netherlands. I am grateful to both of these institutions.

There are many ways to find financing for competitions. Ask officials at the school you attend, or try the art and education departments at your local city or town hall. State or Federal funds may also be available. There are also possibilities of finding sponsorship from corporate institutions, maybe those where your parents are working. There are also art groups and art societies in many towns that would consider helping you with competition expenses. My suggestion is to ask everyone you can think of, if not for direct financial help, then for advice and ideas about securing it.

with jury member Scott Tenant
at Stotsenberg International Guitar Competition in Malibu, CA, 1999.

International Competitions and Prizes I Have Won

-1st prize at the International Guitar Competition "Jacinto e Inocencio Guerrero,"-Madrid, Spain, 1993

-1st prize at the International Guitar Festival IGF-Frechen, Germany, 1995

-1st prize at the International Guitar Competition "Rene Bartoli"-Aix en Provence, France, 1995

-1st prize, special prize for the best interpretation of the works by F. Tárrega and prize of the public at the International Guitar Competition "Francisco Tárrega"-Benicasim, Spain, 1995

-1st prize at the International Guitar Competition "Manufacturas Alhambra"- Alcoy, Spain, 1996

-1st prize at the International Guitar Competition "Printemps de la Guitarre"- Walcourt, Brussels, Belgium, 1996

-1st prize at the Link Music competition- Tilburg, Netherlands, 1997

-1st prize at the International Guitar Foundation of America Competition (GFA), Montreal, Canada, 1998

-1st prize at the Schadt String Competition-Allentown, PA, USA, 1999

-1st prize at the Stotsenberg International Guitar Competition- Malibu, CA, USA, 1999

-2nd prize at the International Guitar Competition "Andrés Segovia"-La Herradura, Spain, 1993

-2nd prize at the International Guitar Competition "Andrés Segovia"-La Herradura, Spain, 1994

-2nd prize at the International Guitar Competition "Andrés Segovia"-La Herradura, Spain, 1995

-2nd prize at the International Guitar Competition "Andrés Segovia"-La Herradura, Spain, 1996

-2nd prize at the International Guitar Competition "Manufacturas Alhambra"-Alcoy, Spain, 1994

-2nd prize and prize of the public at the International Guitar Competition of Tredrez-Locquemeau, France, 1998

-2nd prize at the McMahon International Music Competition, Lawton, OK, USA 2000

-3rd prize at the International guitar competition "Andrés Segovia", Palma de Mallorca, Spain, 1993

-3rd prize at the International guitar competition "Andrés Segovia", Palma de Mallorca, Spain, 199

-3rd prize at the International Guitar Competition "Printemps de la Guitarre"- Walcourt, Brussels, Belgium, 1994

-3rd prize at the International Guitar Competition in Markneukirchen, Germany, 1997

-5th prize at the International Guitar Competition "Printemps de la Guitarre"- Walcourt, Brussels, Belgium, 1994

- Audience award at the International Guitar Competition "Francisco Tárrega"-Benicasim, Spain, 1993

- Special prize at the ARD competition, Munich, Germany, 1993

Of all the prizes I have won there is one that I enjoyed the most because it was the longest lasting. That was the Guitar Foundation of America International Guitar Competition I won in Montreal, Canada in 1998. Part of the first prize was a 58-concert tour in the USA and Canada. An article reflecting on my GFA tour was published on my web site and I am including it on the following pages as well.

1999-2000 GFA Tour Reflections

When I was waiting for the final results of the GFA International Competition, in Montreal, Canada, in1998, my heart was beating very hard because one thing mattered to me a lot: the GFA tour. I did not care so much about the rest of the prize, but I wanted the tour so badly. After the 30 or so international competitions I had taken part in by then, the only thing I could think of was the possibility to play more than 50 concerts in one year all over the US and Canada. No other competition offered such an opportunity. Winning the GFA competition felt like the first time I won an international competition, "Jacinto e Inocencio Guerrero" in Madrid, in 1993. The first time is always the greatest, but getting the 1st prize at GFA was something special.

My GFA tour began in October 1999, the 2nd of October to be precise. During the summer of 1999 I was in touch with Bob Mayeur, the GFA tour director, providing the promotional material and other things necessary for the tour. I also got in touch with some of my friends, previous winners of the GFA competition, Antigoni Goni and Fabio Zanon, asking for advice and tips about the tour; they were very kind to help me. Also, I heard some stories about the GFA tour from other sources, some of which proved to be true (like having a really full schedule), and others which proved to be wrong.

So, as I said, my touring started in October, and I really enjoyed it. I traveled, played, taught, and not much more… It was really very busy and there was very little time to do anything else. People kept telling me that I'd have a chance to see the USA, but what I really saw were US airports. Sometime there were 4-5 concerts in a row, day after day, which meant taking one, two and sometimes three flights to come to the place where I had to perform, having a nap, play a concert, and the next day the same thing. I also remember people asking me if I was getting tired of playing the same program so many times. I only got tired by the end of the tour, around mid March, and I did change the program on a few occasions. I felt as if every concert was a new experience, which it really was. It was interesting for me to see how one piece would work on different evenings and how the people would react differently to the same piece. I felt better with the performance of a certain piece on one day than on another. One day was best for Ponce, the next day for Rodrigo, another for Asencio and so on…

I had a break at the end of October, then for the Thanksgiving Holiday and a long break for Christmas (about a month). I was glad to go back home to see and be with my wife, but I was also excited to go on the next leg of the tour. The spring part of the tour, as they call it, really began at the end of January, and lasted until mid March with three days break at the beginning of February. In February I was playing in Canada where you can imagine it was very cold and my guitar cracked. My next stop after Canada was Portland, Oregon. Jeff Eliot, famous guitar maker from Portland, offered to help me with my guitar, but he only had few hours after my concert to do so, because the next morning I had a plane to catch. I am very thankful for his help.

I really did not have any unpleasant experiences during the tour, and I only missed one connection in all my flights, which resulted in a cancelled master-class. All other master-classes and 58 concerts went according to the schedule. I always had my schedule listing: people who had to pick me up and phone numbers of those people, as well as phone numbers of the tour director and travel agent responsible for plane tickets. Everything really worked very well. I knew that I had to phone the presenters myself just to be sure that we had the same information about my flight and time of arrival. This kind of information tends to get lost or changed when there are too many people involved. That is just the nature of things, not anybody's fault. Anyway, I do not have any complaints about the organizational part of tour, just the opposite.

Another thing I remember about the tour was experiencing different accommodations. I was lodged in places that varied from the Red Carpet Motel to Fairmont Hotel, and in private homes where sometimes I would have half the house to myself; other times, a family would give me their little daughter's room full of toys and dolls. I enjoyed it all. (I did not play with the toys and dolls but did play video games.)

One of the most controversial issues, which I have heard before about the GFA tour, was the financial part of it. I must admit I was also bothered with that, since the fee paid to the guitarist is very low. I came to understand, however, that you could look at the situation from two perspectives. When you see a bottle that is filled with water up to the middle, one can say it is half empty or half full. It is your choice how you want to put it. That is how I see the issue of the GFA tour fee. I learned to look at it as a bottle half full. And not only that, but it keeps filling up! If you take a time to think about the GFA, you will realize that this is the organization which in about 18 years managed to put a competition that at this point has the best 1st prize among the guitar competitions. It is true that you do not earn enough money during 7-8 months of touring to be comfortable financially, but remember what the 1st prize was 15 years ago, and then think what it is today and what it will be in 5-10 years from now. GFA is improving the competition every year and the 50–60 concerts they organize for the winner is the best opportunity a young performer can get.

The tour gave me an incredible experience and most of all it gave me the chance that I wanted: to play and show people what I could do. That is the best thing anyone can give us professionally, to allow us to show what we can do. I enjoyed the tour immensely, I gained experience regarding the intense touring (and I hope it never gets so intense again), and it allowed me to create contacts with the presenters, or in other words, it really put me on the guitar concert stages of the USA and Canada. I am in every way thankful to the GFA for organizing this competition and the tour. I wish them all the best for the future, and I hope they also keep up with the good work. To those who think about taking part in the GFA competition, I can say it is most definitely worth a try. As for the sponsors of GFA, I hope you'll keep supporting this organization and consider writing a bigger check.

with jury members David Leisner (left), Carlos Barbosa Lima (right)
and finalists Rene Izquierdo (second left) and Luiz Mantovani (middle)
at the Schadt String Competition in Allentown, PA-1999.

List of International Guitar Competitions

CERTAMEN INTERNACIONAL DE GUITARRA CLASSICA
"ANDRÉS SEGOVIA"
OFICINAS MUNICIPALES DE LA HERRADURRA
C/GONZALO BARBERO No 1
18697 LA HERRADURA –ALMUNECAR
GRANADA
SPAIN
TEL: 34 58 64 04 25
FAX: 34 58 82 77 94   /   34 58 63 43 03
JANUARY 2-6

CONCERT ARTIST GUILD
850 SEVENTH AVENUE, SUITE 1205
NEW YORK, NY 10019-5230
TEL: 1-212-333-5200
FAX: 1-212-977-7149
E-MAIL: CAGuild@aol.com
FEBRUARY (annually for all instruments together)

YOUNG CONCERT ARTIST, INC.
250 WEST 57 STREET
NEW YORK, NY 10019, USA
TEL: 1 212 307 6655
FAX: 1 212 581 8894
FOR ALL INSTUMENTS (Annual)

The Stosenberg International Classical Guitar Competition
P.O. Box 6253
MALIBU, CALIFORNIA 90265
USA
TEL: 1-818-889-2660
FAX: 1-818-889-2806
PRIZES: 1st-$10,000; 2nd-$3,500; 3rd-$1,500; 4th & 5th-$1,000
Odd-numbered years in June

INTERNATIONAL ANNA AMALIA GUITAR COMPETITION WEIMAR
HOCHSCHULE FUR MUSIK "FRANZ LISZT" WEIMAR
PLATZ DER DEMOKRATIE 2/3 99423 WEIMAR-GERMANY
TEL: 49 3643 555150   FAX: 49 3642 61865

CONCURSO INTERNACIONAL DE GUITARRA "MANUEL PONCE"
COLINA 47, LOMAS DE BEZARES
MEXICO, D.F. 11910
FAX: 570 5113
E-mail: corazon@mpsnet.com.mx
MARCH (annually)

INTERNATIONAL GUITAR FESTIVAL FRECHEN
JENS KIENBAUM
JULICHER STR. 24
50674 KOLN-GERMANY
TEL: 49 221 242283
MARCH –APRIL (Annually)

CONCURSO INTERNACIONAL DE GUITARRA "ALHAMBRA"
MANUFACTURAS ALHAMBRA, S.L.
C/DUQUESA DE ALMODOVAR, 11
03830-MURO DE ALCOY – SPAIN
TEL: 34 6 553011 FAX: 34 6 553 0190 / 34 6 6516302
YUKI-ORGANIZACIÓN: 34 6 5337517
EVERY TWO YEARS IN APRIL

INTERNATIONAL COMPETITION "MARIA CANALS"
ARS NOVA-CONCURSO MARI CANALS
GRAN VIA DE LES CORTS CATALANS 654, PRAL.,
08010 BARCELONA – SPAIN
TEL & FAX: 34 3 318 77 31
APRIL-MAY, EVERY 5-6 YEARS

CONCORSO ITERNAZIONALE DE CHITARRA
ACADEMIA DE LA CHITARRA
VIA VITO SANSONETTI 64
74017 MOTTOLA (TA)-ITALY
TEL 099 880 95 41 Mr. VITTA TORELI
JUNE

SHELL DARWIN INTERNATIONAL GUITAR COMPETITION
NORTHERN TERRITORY UNIVERSITY
SCHOOL OF MUSIC
DARWIN NT 0909 AUSTRALIA
ADRIAN WALTER, DIRECTOR
TEL: 61 8 8946 6419
FAX: 61 8 8946 6540
E-MAIL: ad_walter@bligh.ntu.edu.au
JUNE 30- JULY 9

CONCOURS INTERNACIONAL DE GUITARE DE RENE BARTOLI
8, SQUARE DES TISSERANDS
13111 CODOUX – FRANCE
TEL: 42 52 03 79
FAX: 42 52 06 58
FIRST WEEK OF JULY (ANNUALLY)

CONCOURS INTERNACIONAL DE GUITARE MAIRIE,
22300 TREDREZ-LOCQUEMEAU, FRANCE
TEL: 02 96 35 74 52
FAX: 02 96 35 75 91
JULY 7-13

CONCORSO INTERNACIONALE DI CHITARRA CLASSICA
"MICHELE PITTALUGA" PREMIO CITTA DI ALESSANDRIA
PIAZZA GARIBALDI, 16
15100 ALESSANDRIA
ITALY
TEL: 39-131-251207
FAX: 39-131-235507
E-mail: pittalug@email.alessandria.alpcom.it
SEPTEMBER (ANNUALLY)

CONCURSO INTERNACIONAL DE GUITARRA "FRANCISCO TÁRREGA"
AYUNTAMIENTO DE BENICASIM, MEDICO SEGARRA 4
12560 BENICASIM (CS)
SPAIN
TEL: (34 64) 30 09 62, 30 38 51
FAX: (34-64) 30 34 32
END OF AUGUST/ BEGINNING OF SEPT.-ANNUALLY

INTERNATIONAL GUITAR COMPETITION KARL SCHEIT
HOCHSCHULE FUR MUSIK UND DARSTELLENDE KUNST IN WIEN
JOHANNESGASSE 8,A-1010 VIENNA, AUSTRIA
TEL & FAX 43 1 51596 264

INTERNATIONAL GUITAR COMPETITION "DE BONIS"
TEATRO "A. RENDANO"
SEGRETARIA DEL CONCORSO "DE BONIS"
PIAZZA XV MARZO
87100 COSENZA
ITALY
TEL: 39 984 81322079
FAX: 39 984 81374165
SEPTEMBER

"PRINTEMPS DE LA GUITARE"
PLACE DE CHEF-LIEU,9
B-6040 CHARLEROI JUMET
BELGIUM
TEL: 32 71 35 04 48
FAX: 32 71 35 53 20
SEPTEMBER- OCTOBER (EVERY 2 YEARS)

CONCORSO INTERNAZIONALI DI CHITARRA CLASSICA
"MAURO GIULIANI"
GIOVANI ANTONIONI, CHIEF OFFICIER
VIA SPARANO 141
70121 BARI
ITALY
TEL: 39 80 521 1908
FAX: 39 80 523 7154
OCTOBER (ANNUALLY)

GFA
JEFF COGAN
7337 E. SADDLEHORN WAY
ORANGE CA 92869
USA
TEL: 1-714-289-1472
www.guitarfoundation.org
OCTOBER (ANNUALLY)

INT. GUITAR CONTEST "HEITOR VILLA LOBOS "
MUSEU VILLA LOBOS
RUA SOROCABA 200, BOTAFOGO
22271 RIO DE JENEIRO RJ
BRAZIL
TEL: 021 266 3845
FAX: 021 266 3894
E-MAIL: mvillalobos@ax.ibase.org.br
NOVEMBER 13-18

INTERNATIONAL GUITAR COMPETTION "ANDRÉS SEGOVIA"
C/RAMON LLULL 2 , C/O CAIXA DE BALEARS "SA NOSTRA"
07001 PALMA DE MALLORCA
TEL: 34 71 71 4141
FAX: 34 71 72 83 44
NOVEMBER, EVERY 2 YEARS, last in '95,not in '97

CONCURSO INTERNACIONAL DE GUITARRA "FUNDACION GUERRERO"
GRAN VIA,78
28013 MADRID
SPAIN
TEL: 34 1 547 6618
FAX: 34 1 548 3493
NOVEMBER EVERY 2 YEARS, LAST IN 1996

CONCOUR INTERNATIONAL D'EXECUTION MUSICALE DR. LUIS SIGAL
DIRECCIÓN DEL CONCURSO
CALLE ARLEGUI No 683, CASILLA 31-D
VINA DEL MAR
CHILE
TEL: 56 32 88 33 58
FAX: 56 32 68 06 33
NOVEMBER 8-15, GUITAR IN 1999

CONCORSO INTERNACIONALE DI CHITARRA CLASSICA
"CIVITAS MUSICAE"
CITTA DELLA PIEVE
PALAZZO BAGLIONI
LARGO BAGLIONI
06062 CITTA DELLA PIEVE (PG)
ITALY
TEL: 39 578 299 339
DECEMBER

TOKYO INTERNATIONAL GUITAR CONTEST
JAPAN FEDERATION OF GUITARISTS
4-44-7-13, CHUOH, NAKANO-KU, TOKYO164
JAPAN
TEL: 81-3-3383-1819
TAPE BEFORE JULY 31ST
DECEMBER, ANNUALLY

For more information on competitions, visit www.musicalamerica.com and www.worldguitarist.com

Denis Azabagic

Photo: Javier Albella-Spain

Born in Tuzla, Bosnia/Herzegovina, in November 1972, Denis Azabagic is considered one of the best guitarists of his generation. He holds more than 20 awards from international competitions. In 1993, at the age of 20, he became the youngest winner of one of the most prestigious International Guitar Competitions "Jacinto e Inocencio Guerrero," in Madrid, Spain. After listening to Azabagic, distinguished Spanish composer, Anton Garcia Abril said: "I am sure that with time, he is going to be one of the greatest guitarist of the world." After his success in Madrid, Denis has maintained a prize-winning position in virtually every competition he has participated in.

In 1993 Denis formed a duo with his wife, Eugenia Moliner Ferrer, a flutist, and since then they have played concerts and festivals throughout Europe and the USA. Today known as the Cavatina Duo, they have recorded their first CD for the Spanish label Opera Tres. As a soloist Denis has played with various orchestras, and he has given recitals in Europe and the United States. Denis has published two CDs, one for Printemps de la guitarre and another for Opera Tres.

Denis has recorded six CDs for international labels such as Opera Tres, Printemps de la guitarre and Naxos, as well as a video for Mel Bay Publications. As a soloist, Denis has appeared in the US with the Allentown Symphony, Charlotte Symphony, Savannah Symphony, and in Europe with Orchestre Royal de chambre de Mons and Symphony Orchestra of Madrid, among others. He played as a guest performer at several venues such as Masters of the Guitar at the Royal Concertgebouw in Netherlands, Radio France in Paris, France, Aix en Provence Festival, France, El Palau de la Musica, Valencia-Spain, Savannah on Stage, USA, Omni Foundation, USA, etc. In 2002 he was appointed to the faculty of the Chicago College for Performing Arts (Roosevelt University) in downtown Chicago.

Made in the USA
San Bernardino, CA
07 September 2015